WORMS OF WISDOM

by
Patricia Martin
&
Peter Mason

Logo and Cover Art
Richard Skiermont

Copyright © 1992 Great Quotations, Inc.

All rights reserved. No part of this publication may be reproduced or transmitted in any form or by any means, electronic or mechanical, including photocopy, recording, or an information storage and retrieval system, without the written permission of the publisher.

ISBN 1-56245-050-6

DEDICATION

This book is dedicated to all who *DARE*
to be cosmic rebels
philosophers, and fools.

—Patricia Martin

For Tracey, Daniel, Christine, and Kimberly.
Dedicated to those who
conceived of, built, and maintain Salisbury Cathedral
and everyone else not named Rocco.

—Peter Mason

BARKING UP

THE WRONG THREE

SCREAM WINDOWS

THE GRIM PEEPER

ROW ROW ROW YOUR GOAT

THE MOUNTIES ALWAYS

GET THEIR TAN

LONDON BRITCHES

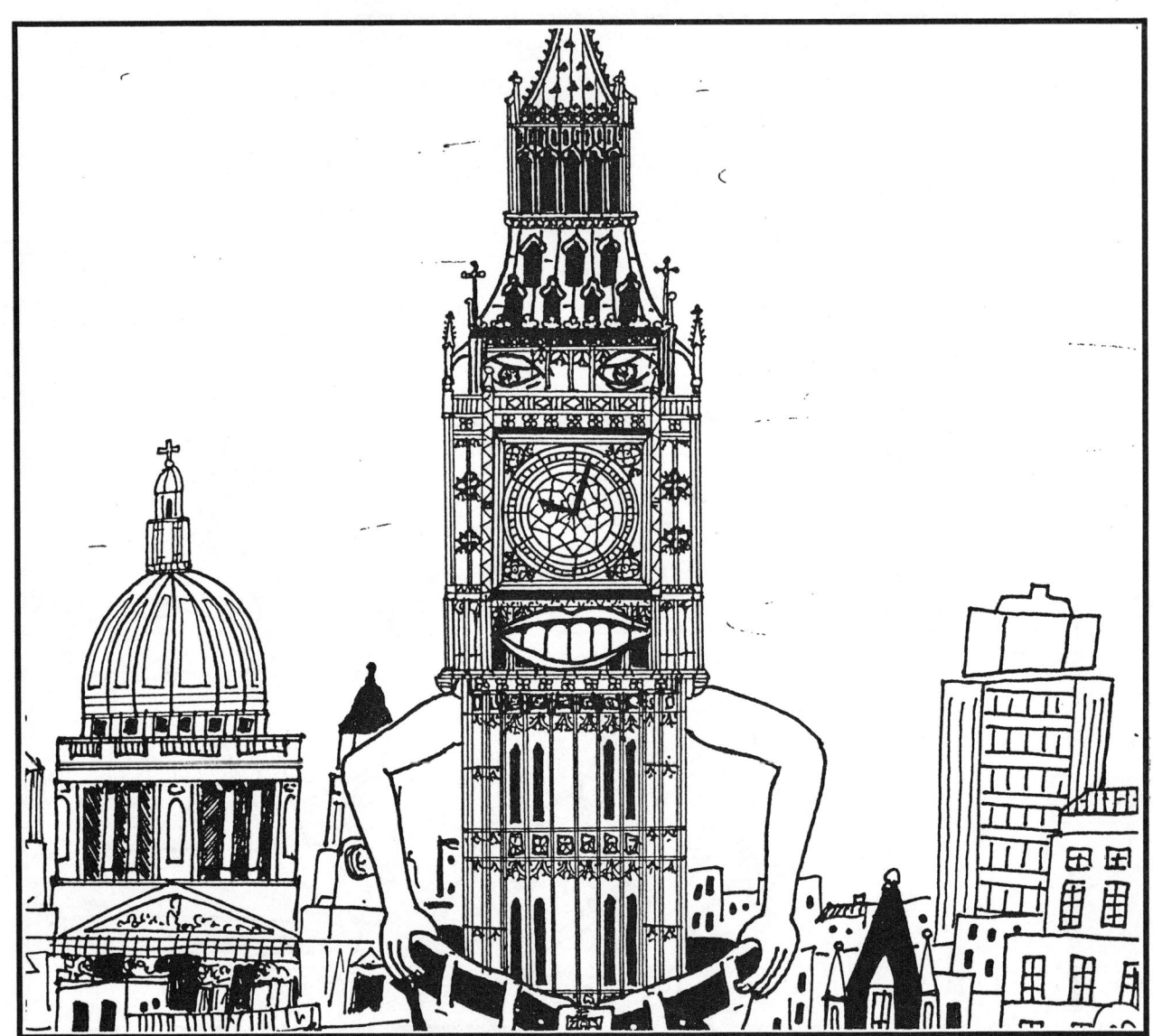

FALLING DOWN

A SLUMBERJACK

A FEAR OF KITES

YOU CAN'T SEASON

WITH A WARPED MIND

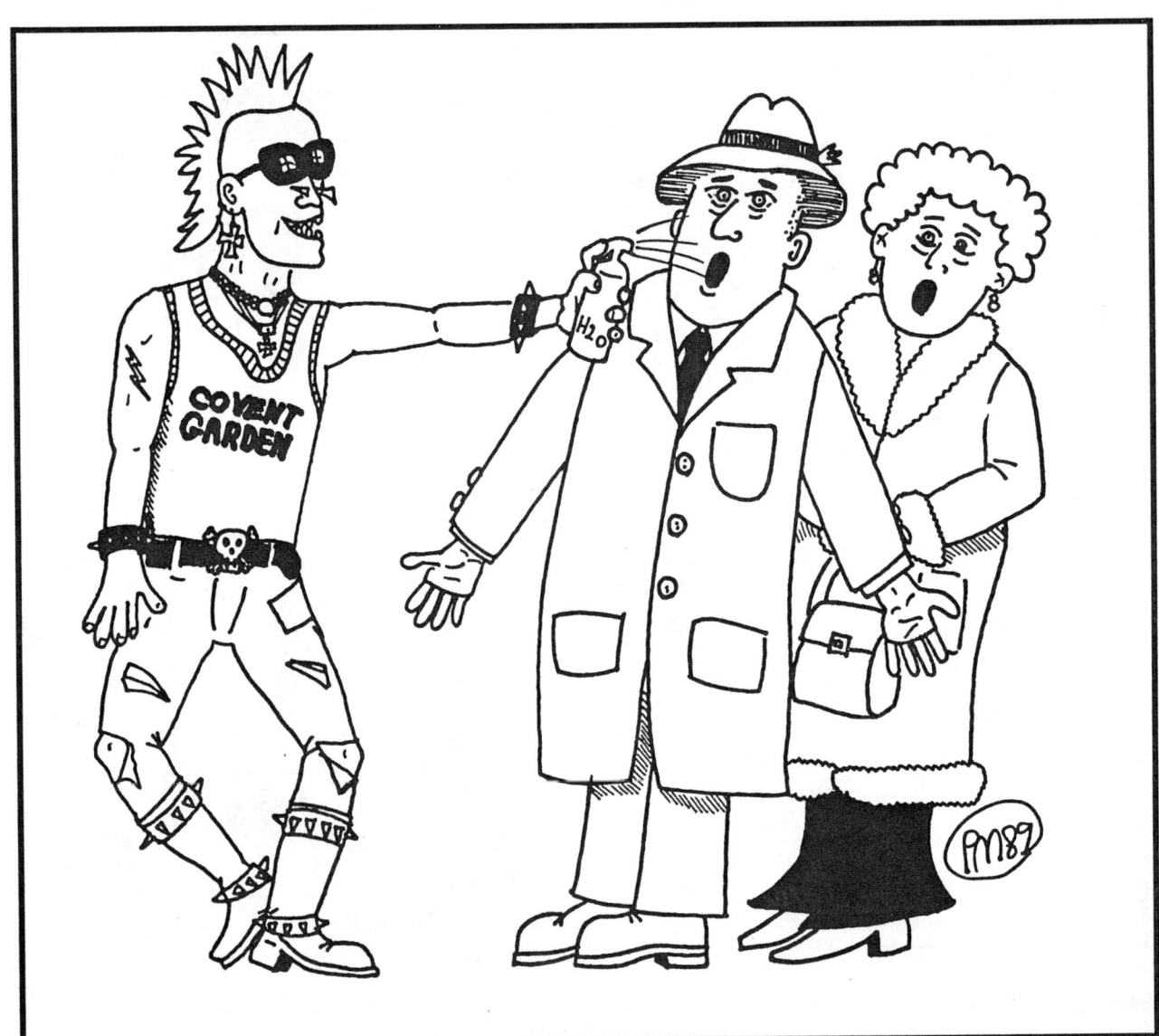

SPRAYED BY A PUNK

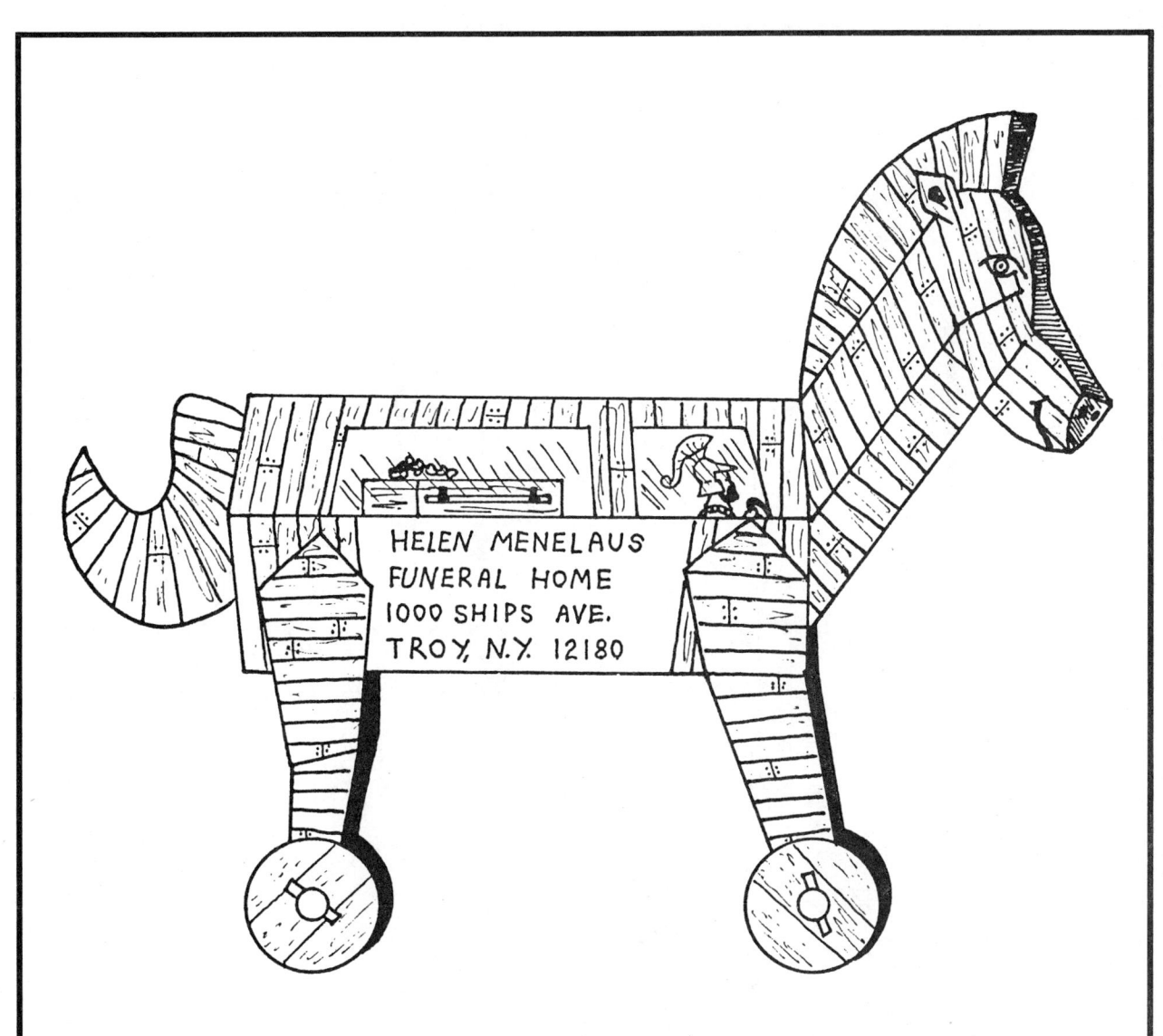

THE TROJAN HEARSE

THE GLASS IS ALWAYS

CLEANER ON THE OTHER SIDE OF THE FENCE

HE FLOATS THROUGH THE AIR

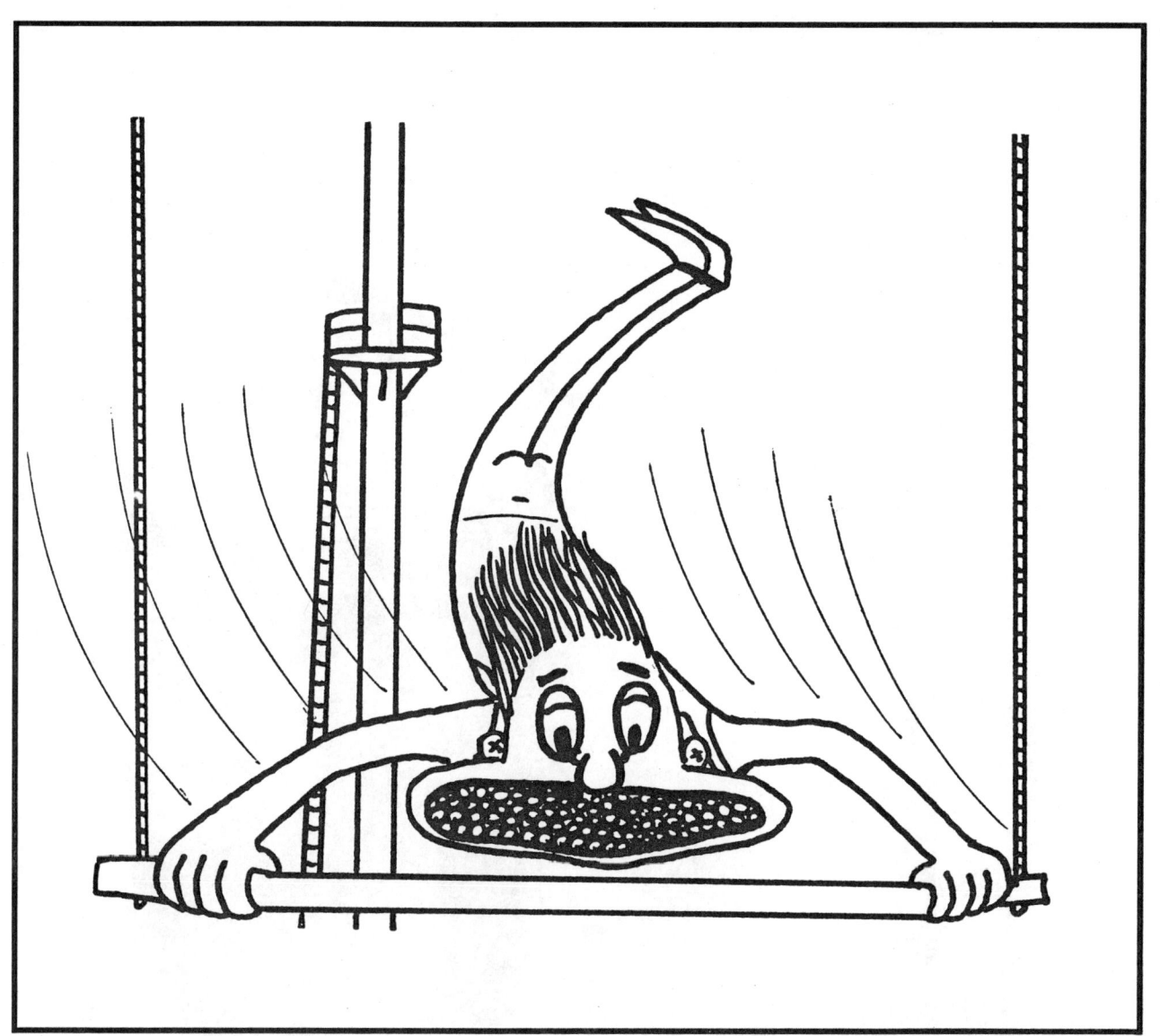

WITH A MOUTHFUL OF PEAS, THE DARING YOUNG MAN ON THE FLYING TRAPEZE

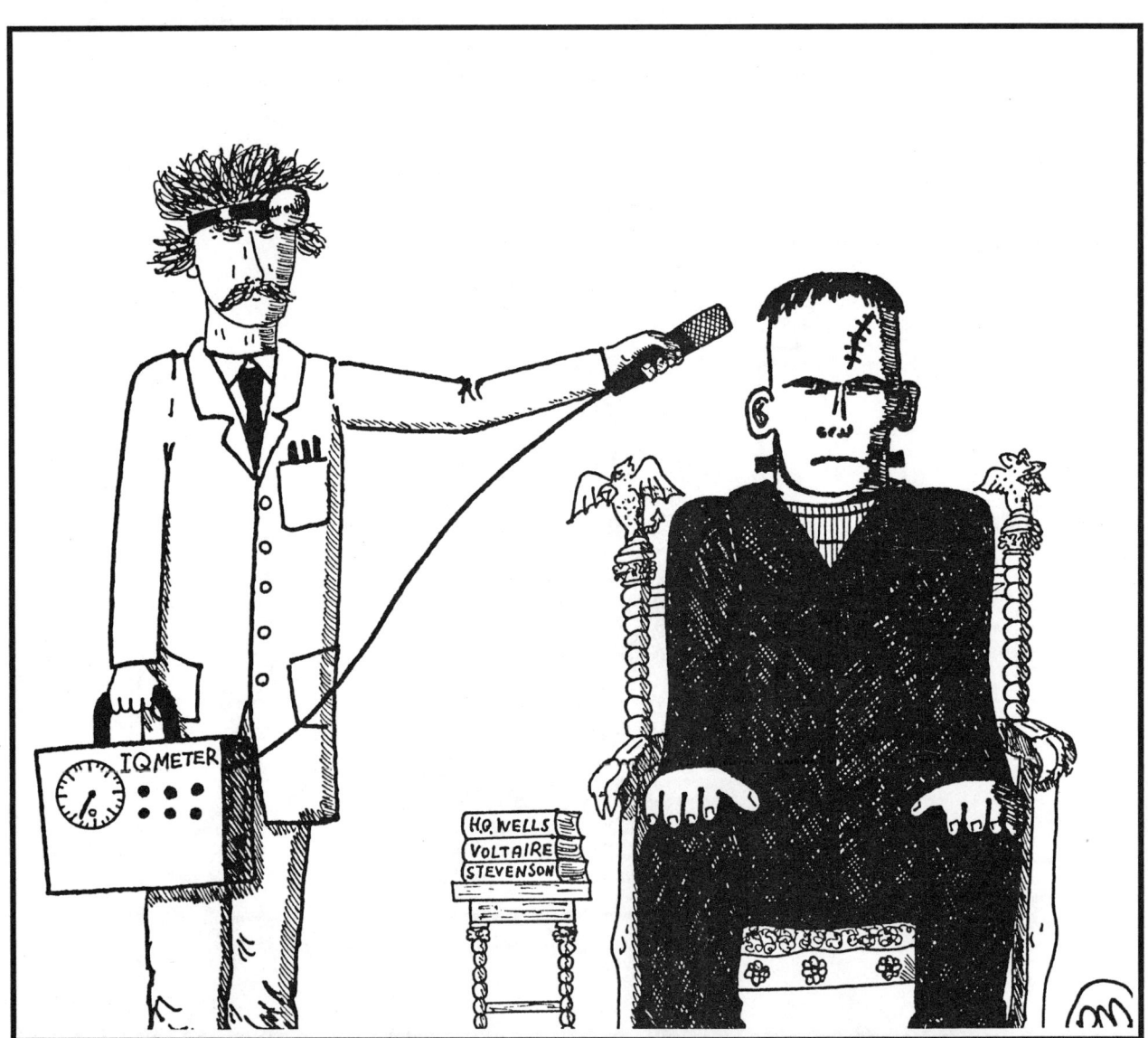

MENTAL DETECTOR

DOWN ON HIS TRUCK

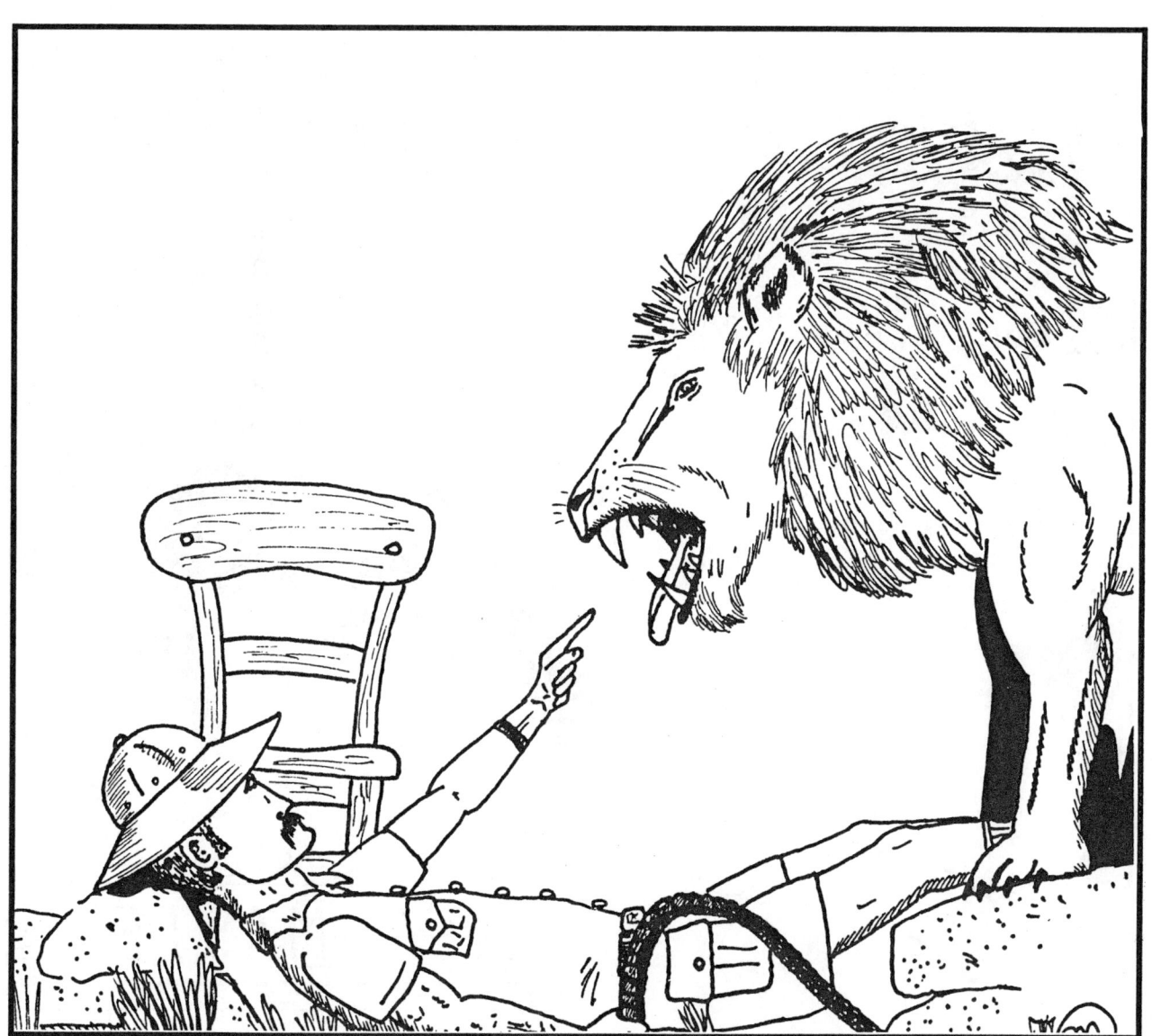

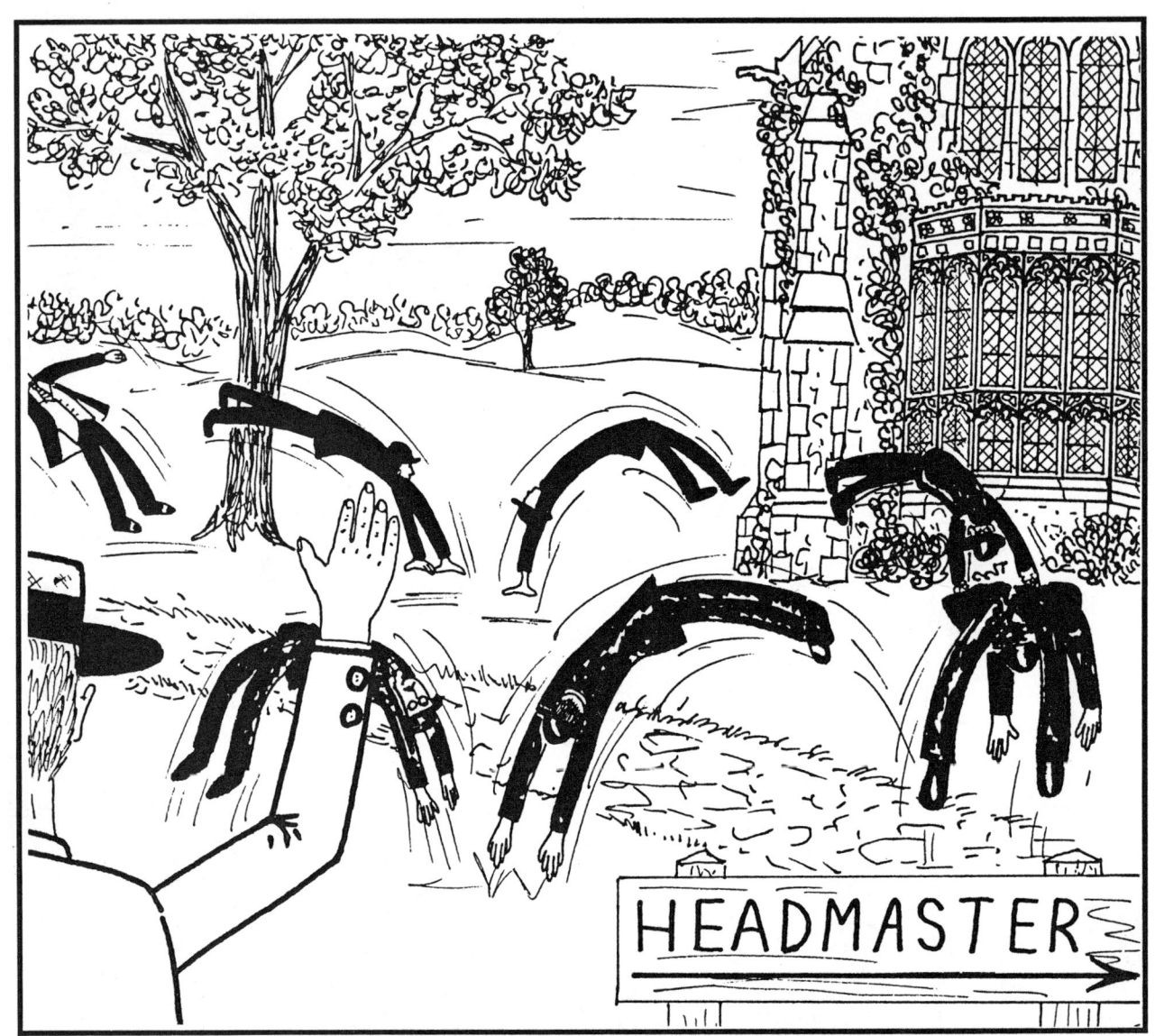

GOOD-BYE MR. FLIPPS

BLESSED ARE THE

CHEESEMAKERS

METAL ANGUISH

SHE GAVE HIM A BEERFUL

DOCTOR LIVE IN STONE

I PRESUME

I GET NO KICK

FROM CHAMPLAIN

FALL OF THE ROMAN UMPIRE

BATS OFF TO LARRY

TEQUILA MOCKINGBIRD

TO TEE OR NOT TO TEE

A TRANSOM FACE

SEAL OF APPROVAL

HAIR TODAY

GONE TOMORROW

PUBLIC EXCUSE CHANNEL

PHONE IS WHERE

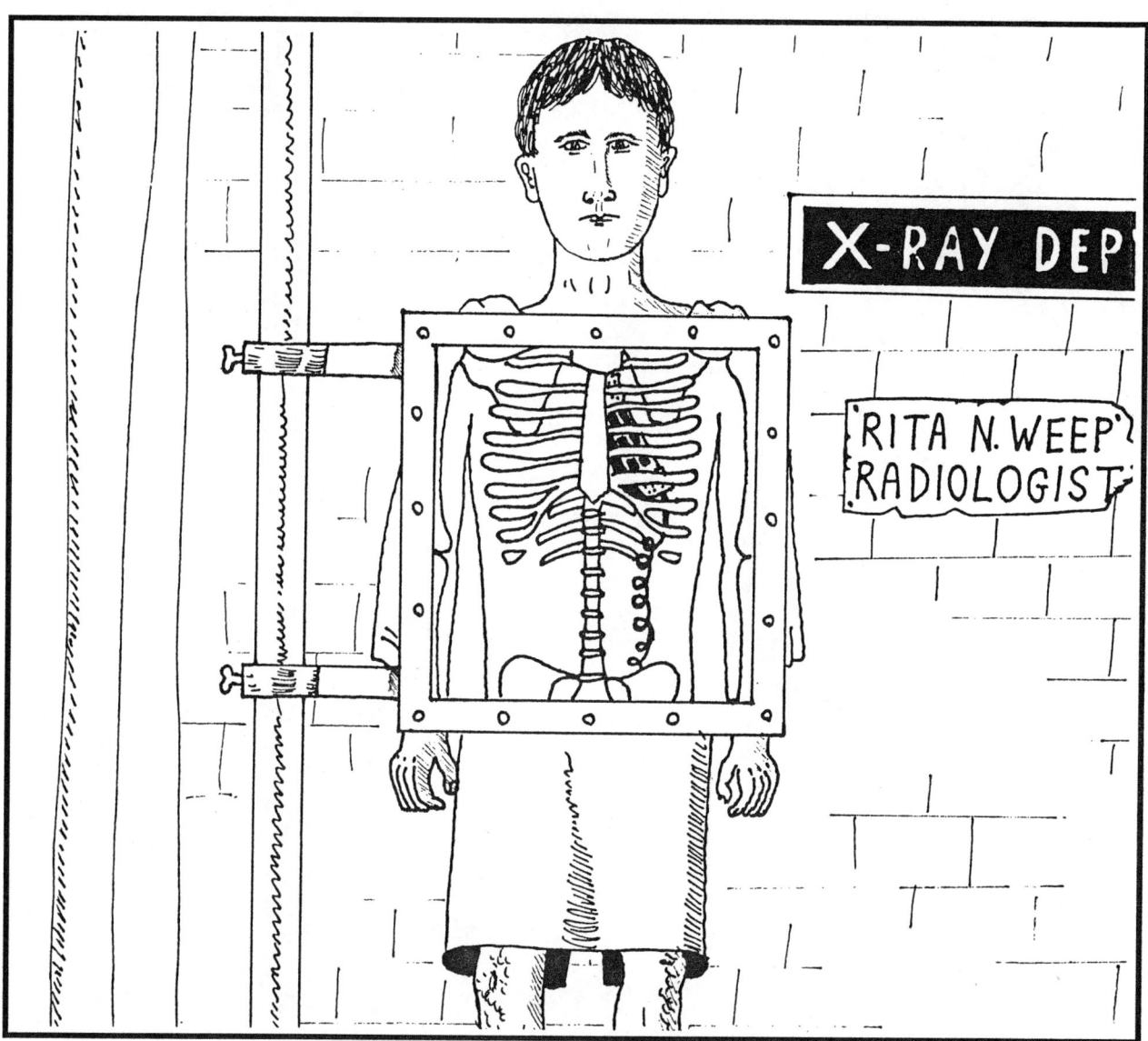

THE HEART IS

TORN BETWEEN

TWO RUBBERS

DON'T GIVE UP

THE CRYPT

A ROADS SCHOLAR

SOME ENSLANTED EVENING

THE ABDOMINAL SNOWMAN

THE WHOLE OF MY WIFE

FLASHED BEFORE MY EYES

A VACUUM CLAMER

I LEFT MY HARP

IN SAN FRANCISCO

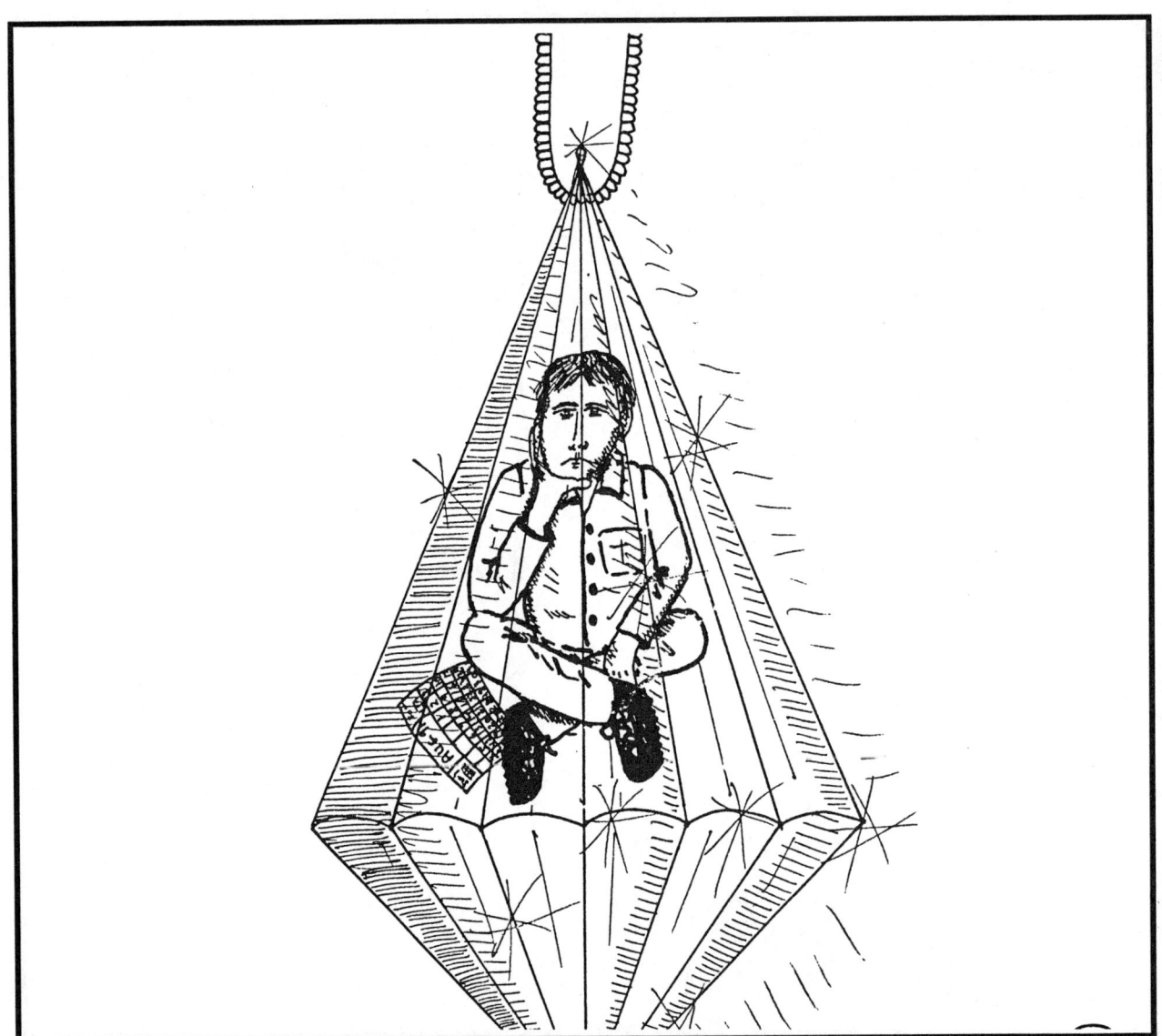

RED SNAILS IN THE SUNSET

SEARCHING FOR

THE LOCHNESS MOBSTER

SCHLOCK ABSORBER

WIFE IMITATING ART

A WOLF IN

SHIPS CLOTHING

A PROPHETABLE IDEA

SHACK IN THE BOX

AHEAD OF HIS DIME

PHONE, PHONE

ON THE RANGE

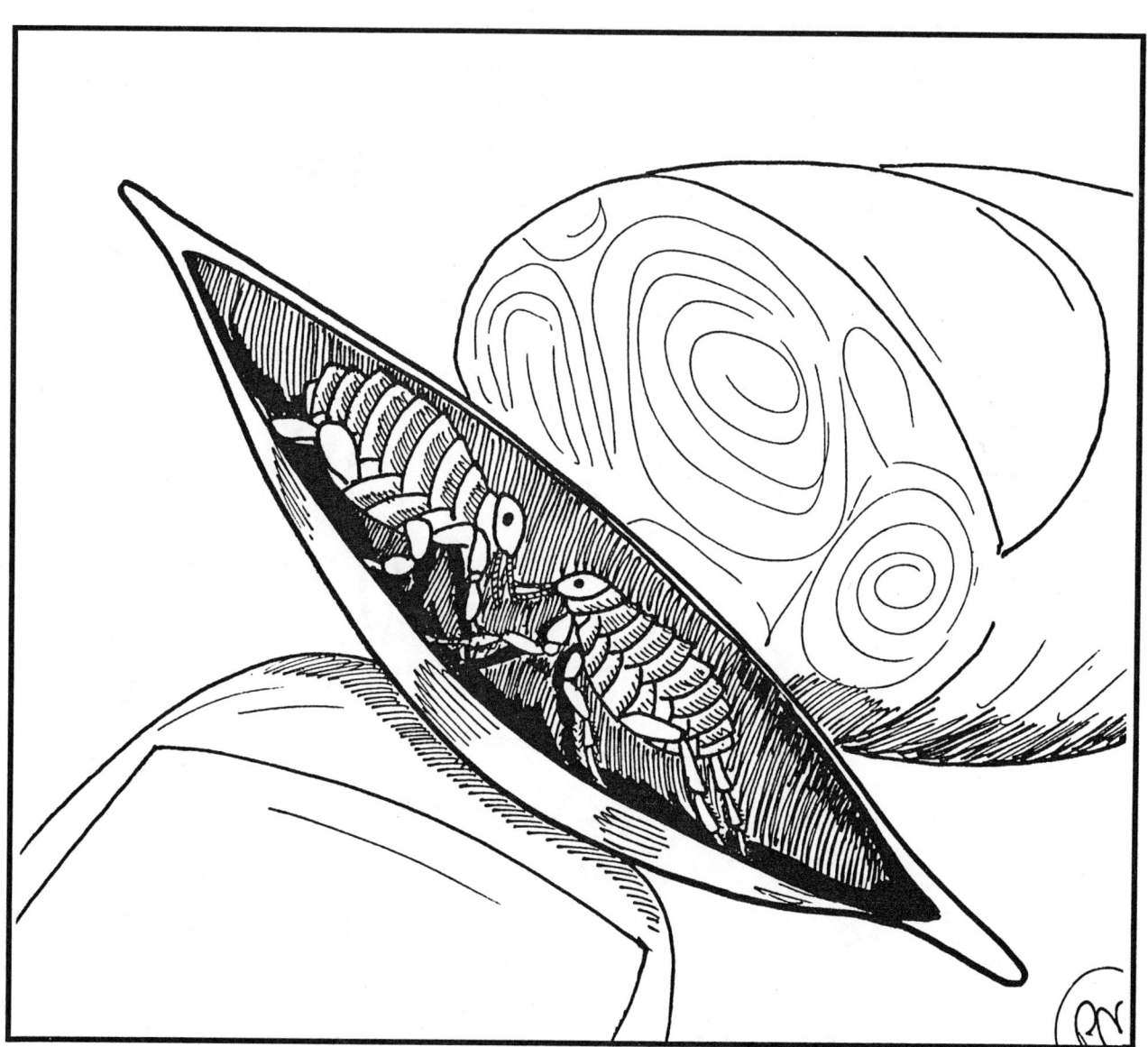

TWO FLEAS IN A POD

WHEREVER HE HANGS HIS

RAT IS HIS HOME

DEAD MEN TELL NO WHALES

TWO FISH ENTERING

NOAH'S SHARK

SPOON RIVER

HOT CROSS NUNS

ABUSEMENT PARK

PUTTING ALL HIS

LEGS IN ONE BASKET

SMILE, YOU'RE

ON CANYON CAMERA

NIGHT OF THE LIVING BREAD

CRYING OVER DRILLED MILK

LOOK WHAT

THE HAT DRAGGED IN

DRIVING HER NEW

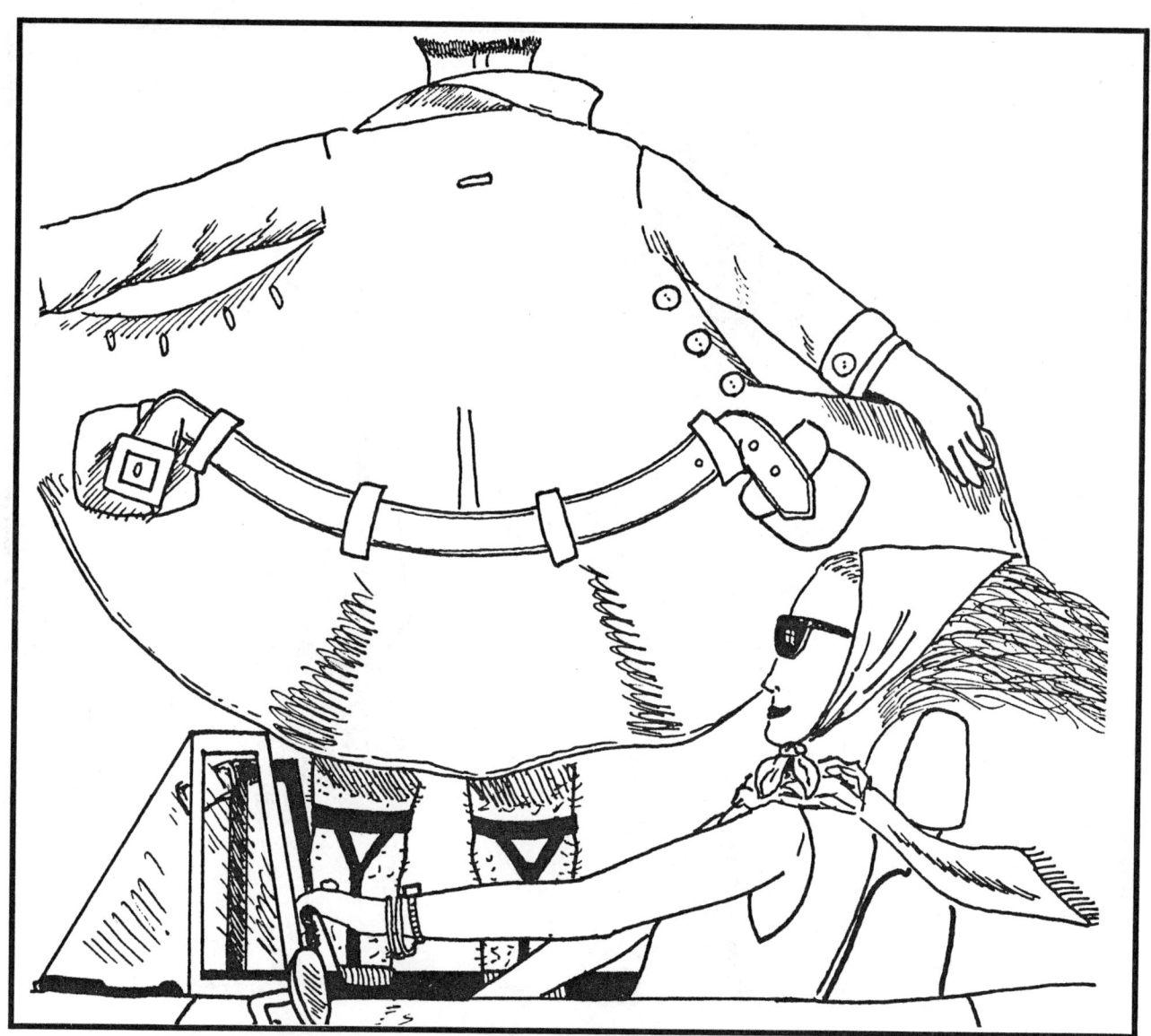

PERVERTABLE

WHEN HAIRY MET SALLY

UNIDENTIFIED

FRYING OBJECT

TENNIS OBOE

NEVER GIVE A SUCKER

AN EVEN RAKE

A DORK IN THE ROAD

THE VENETIAN BLIND

TOOTH DISTRACTION

WE'RE GOING MOUTH

FOR THE WINTER

THE FACE THAT LAUNCHED

A THOUSAND QUIPS

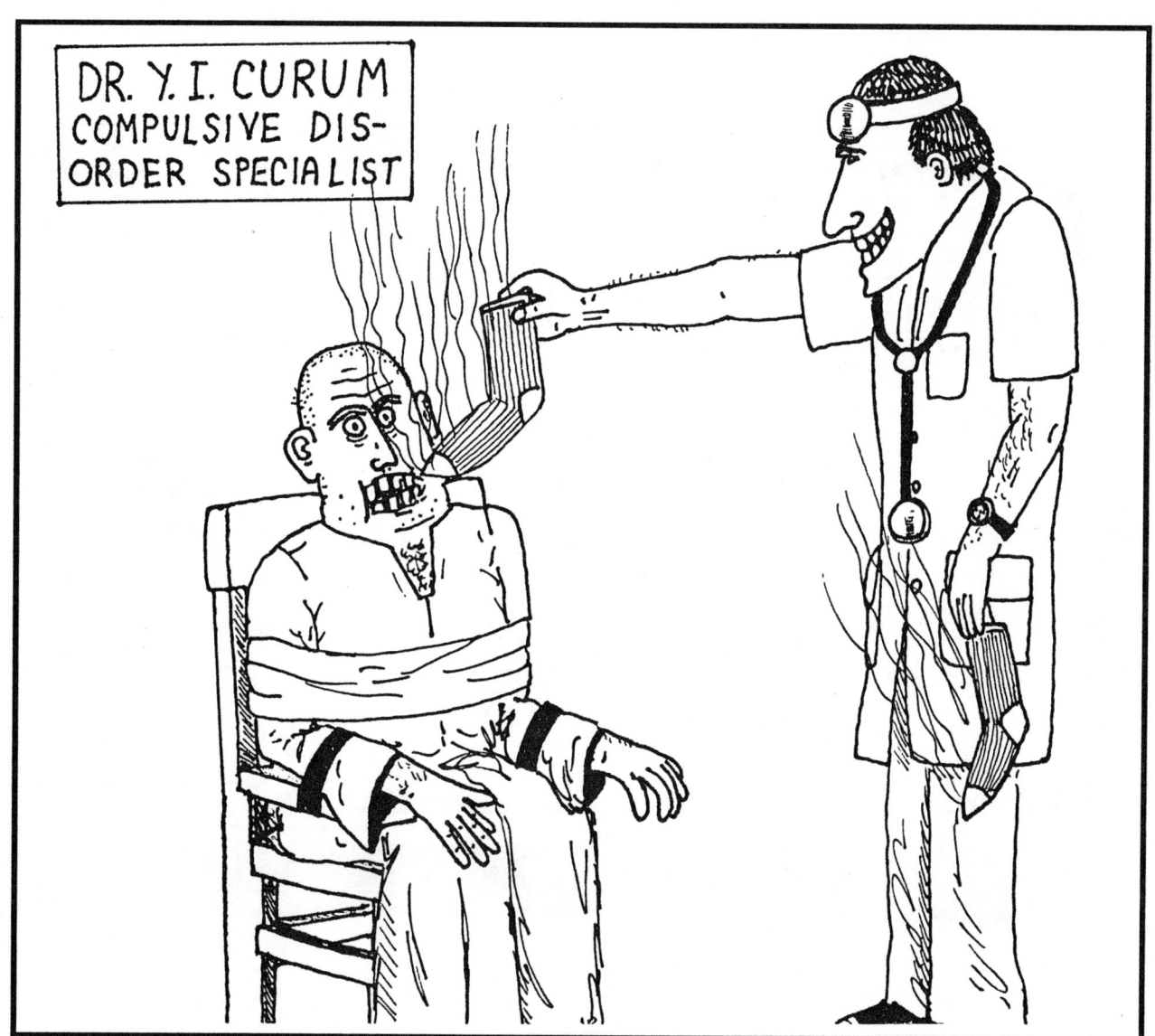

SOCK THERAPY

LADY SINGS THE NEWS

GUNFIGHT AT THE O.K. CANAL

SURVIVAL OF THE FATTEST

NERO PIDDLED WHILE

ROME BURNED